Farmers

Quinn M. Arnold

seedlings

CREATIVE EDUCATION • CREATIVE PAPERBACKS

Published by Creative Education and Creative Paperbacks
P.O. Box 227, Mankato, Minnesota 56002
Creative Education and Creative Paperbacks
are imprints of The Creative Company
www.thecreativecompany.us

Design by Ellen Huber; production by Christine Vanderbeek
Art direction by Rita Marshall
Printed in the United States of America

Photographs by Alamy (Mint Images Limited), iStockphoto
(andrearenata, Avalon_Studio, Nikada, Olha_stock, oticki,
stevanovicigor, Ron_Thomas, valio84sl), Shutterstock (Alena
Brozova, Svetlana Foote, kukiat B, Viktor Kunz, MaxyM,
OKAWA PHOTO, Dusan Petkovic, Luis Santos, Igor Stramyk,
Vyacheslav Svetlichnyy, Visionsi)

Library of Congress Cataloging-in-Publication Data
Names: Arnold, Quinn M., author.
Title: Farmers / Quinn M. Arnold.
Series: Seedlings.
Includes bibliographical references and index.
Summary: A kindergarten-level introduction to farmers,
covering their job description, the places where they work, and
how they help the community by growing crops and raising
livestock.
Identifiers: LCCN 2016059802
ISBN 978-1-60818-873-4 (hardcover)
ISBN 978-1-62832-488-4 (pbk)
ISBN 978-1-56660-921-0 (eBook)
Subjects: LCSH: 1. Farmers—Juvenile literature. 2. Farms—
Juvenile literature.
Classification: LCC S519.A75 2017 / DDC 630.92—dc23
CCSS: RI.K.1, 2, 3, 4, 5, 6, 7;
RI.1.1, 2, 3, 4, 5, 6, 7; RF.K.1, 3; RF.1.1

First Edition HC 9 8 7 6 5 4 3 2 1
First Edition PBK 9 8 7 6 5 4 3 2 1

TABLE OF CONTENTS

Hello, farmers!

Farmers raise animals.
They grow crops.
Crops like corn
become food
and fuel.

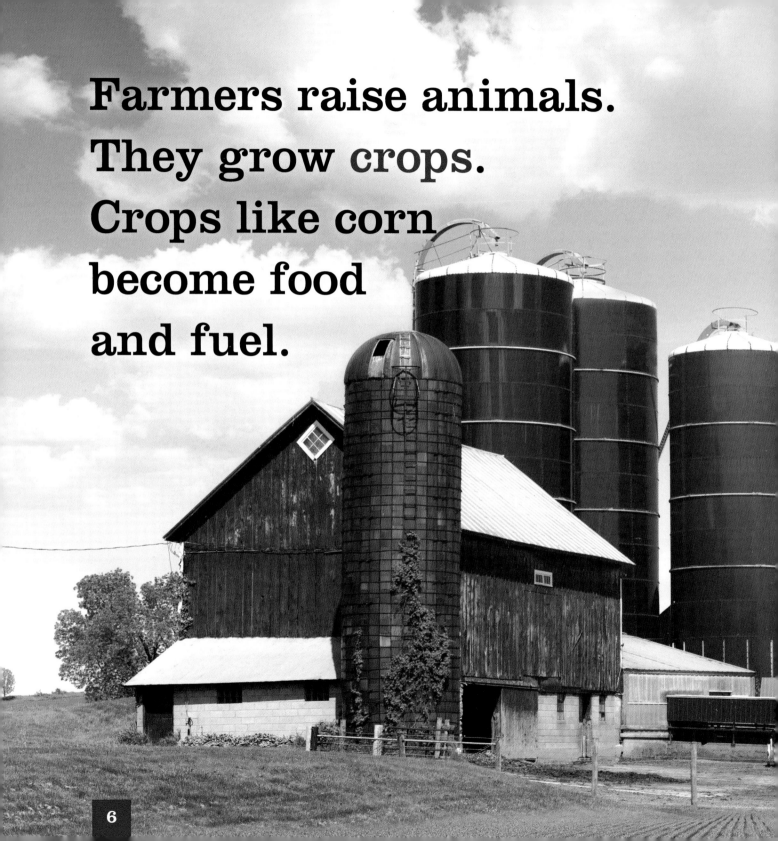

Crops like cotton make clothing.

Farmers plant seeds in big fields. The seeds grow into crops. Then farmers harvest them.

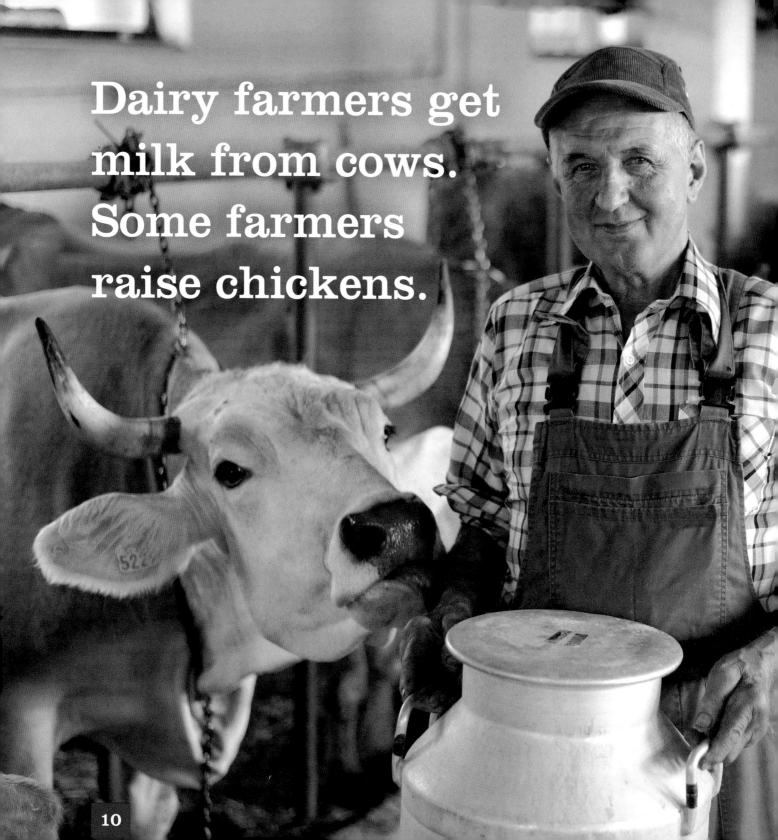

Dairy farmers get milk from cows. Some farmers raise chickens.

They gather chicken eggs.

A farmer plows soil with a tractor. Other machines plant seeds and pick up crops.

Most farmers live and work on farms. They spend a lot of time outside. They fix barns and fences.

Farmers grow and harvest crops.

They take care
of their animals.
They sell food
to people in
communities.

Goodbye, farmers!

Picture a Farmer

farmer

work gloves

work boots

barn

calf

Words to Know

crops: plants that are grown for people and animals to eat

harvest: to gather crops at the end of the growing season

plows: makes land ready for planting by turning over soil

Read More

Meister, Cari. *Farmers.*
Minneapolis: Jump!, 2015.

West, David. *Farm Machinery.*
Mankato, Minn.: Smart Apple Media, 2015.

Websites

Agriculture in the Classroom: Kids' Zone
http://www.agclassroom.org/kids/index.htm
Take quizzes, play games, learn about farms in your state, and more!

My American Farm: Games
http://www.myamericanfarm.org/classroom/games
Play games to learn more about farms and farming.

Index